Rethinking "Budgeting"

How to Escape the Poverty Mindset and Create a Lifestyle That Works for You

By Simeon Lindstrom

Table Of Contents

Introduction

Chapter 1: Why Most Budgeting Advice is Junk

Chapter 2: The Cycle You Never Knew You Were Trapped in

    "Poor": An Expanded Definition

Chapter 3: Three Beliefs That Impoverish You

    Active or Reactive?

    Logical or Emotional?

    Audacious or Doubtful?

    "Entertainment" – A Trap

Chapter 4: What's Your Attitude to Money?

    Money Personality One: The Dreamer

    Money Personality Two: The Emotional Ostrich

    Money Personality Three: The Big Spender

    Money Personality Four: The Money Martyr

    Money Personality Five: The Confident Realist

Chapter 5: Attitudes Lead to Behaviors, which Lead to Attitudes

Chapter 6: This is NOT a Motivational Book

Chapter 7: Breaking the Cycle

    Breaking the cycle if you're The Dreamer

    Breaking the cycle if you're an Emotional Ostrich

- Breaking the cycle if you're a Big Spender
- Breaking the cycle if you're a Money Martyr

Chapter 8: Budget Like A Rich Person
- Get cheap – REALLY cheap – with the things that don't matter to you
- Dream first, then think about the money later
- Stay Focused

Conclusion

© Copyright 2016 by Simeon Lindstrom - All rights reserved.

This document is geared towards providing exact and reliable information in regards to the topic and issue covered. The publication is sold with the idea that the publisher is not required to render accounting, officially permitted, or otherwise, qualified services. If advice is necessary, legal or professional, a practiced individual in the profession should be ordered.

- From a Declaration of Principles which was accepted and approved equally by a Committee of the American Bar Association and a Committee of Publishers and Associations.

In no way is it legal to reproduce, duplicate, or transmit any part of this document in either electronic means or in printed format. Recording of this publication is strictly prohibited and any storage of this document is not allowed unless with written permission from the publisher. All rights reserved.

The information provided herein is stated to be truthful and consistent, in that any liability, in terms of inattention or otherwise, by any usage or abuse of any policies, processes, or directions contained within is the solitary and utter responsibility of the recipient reader. Under no circumstances will any legal responsibility or blame be held against the publisher for any reparation, damages, or monetary loss due to the information herein, either directly or indirectly.

Respective authors own all copyrights not held by the publisher.

The information herein is offered for informational purposes solely, and is universal as so. The presentation of the information is without contract or any type of guarantee assurance.

The trademarks that are used are without any consent, and the publication of the trademark is without permission or backing by the trademark owner. All trademarks and brands within this book are for clarifying purposes only and are the owned by the owners themselves, not affiliated with this document.

Introduction

"We cannot solve our problems with the same thinking we used when we created them."

~ Albert Einstein

This is *not* a book about money. It's a book about *thinking* about money.

In it, you won't find a few quick ways to save a hundred bucks this month or how to cheat the system here and there to save on your utility bills. But what you might find is a new way to think about yourself, the money you make and how it all fits into your broader worldview.

This book in particular was written for those of us who might not have grown up with the right financial role models, or who have ingrained habits that are holding us back. This book is for those of us who grew up poor.

There is a famous Broadway musical currently running that has a lead actress who comes from a severely impoverished Ugandan village. In one scene, she belts out an emotional ballad about how she hopes and dreams about moving to America one day. In her song, she dreams big: imagining that this glorious new city she could live in would have all the vitamin injections you could ever want, warlords who were kind to you and an endless supply of flour at the corner shop.

The song is really funny because the audience knows what she doesn't: that she isn't even able to *think* about something outside her realm of experience. She can't see outside of her mindset. Even her wildest dreams are just a slight variation of her current reality!

Why am I mentioning this? Because so much budget and personal finance advice out there is about solving problems *using the same thinking that created them*. In essence, it's just about being more efficient at keeping yourself stuck in the same old mindset and repeating the same old mistakes. Not about how to actually break away from those mindsets, or learning why exactly you make the mistakes you do.

This is why I won't be making suggestions about how to dilute your fabric softener to save money or how to shop around for interest rates. For the curious, that information is easily available, usually for free.

Instead, this book tries to go a little deeper. It starts with a fact that many personal finance guides out there avoid like the plague: that we are *not* all created equal, we *aren't* all coming from the same place and we're *not* all blessed with a basic, neutral understanding of what money is and how to use it. In fact, most people stay poor not because they don't know to dilute their fabric softener or get the best interest rates. It's because they're *thinking* poor. And they don't know how to think in any other way.

Of course, I'm not suggesting that generations of institutionalized poverty comes down to nothing more than attitude. Certainly, people who've never had the opportunity to develop a different mindset are at a disadvantage. But what I *am* saying is that if you identify as having grown up poor, the only way "out" is to change your mindset. It's beyond this book to explain why you have that mindset to start with, and in most cases, it's nobody's "fault".

Nevertheless, we are all equal in one fundamental way: at every point, no matter who we are or what we've endured in the past, we can make conscious, beneficial decisions for ourselves. No matter what, we can act now in ways that will make tomorrow better than it was today. No matter how broke we are now or how much we've struggled, there's nothing to stop us from stopping, taking control, and *thinking* our way into a different lifestyle, one choice at a time. That's what I hope to show you in the chapters that follow.

Chapter 1: Why Most Budgeting Advice is Junk

I'll never forget the first time I set out to take charge of my own financial life.

I had gotten the idea that drawing up a budget was a good thing that I needed to do. I purchased a book that was popular the time and which promised to teach me all the useful personal finance skills I had never been taught by my parents ...who were frankly horrible with money.

Here's the part where I tell you how poor I grew up. And I did. I'm better off now, but I grew up, like so many other people, barely scraping by. My family lived hand to mouth, we frequently had to do without and money was a constant source of stress and irritation in our home. My parents didn't sort out their retirement properly, we were often in awful debt, and although everyone worked their butts off, we never really seemed to get anywhere. Tale as old as time, right?

But I had just landed my first job, and I decided I wanted to be better than that, and I was going to start with a budget. Very soon, though, it dawned on me: what I was reading wasn't written *for me*. I nearly laughed out loud at the "examples" in this book, the authors giving estimates for stringent household spending that would have felt like Christmas to my family. The authors spoke of financial terms and concepts I had no idea about. I soon felt like a massive loser. Too poor even to budget properly! It hurt.

I read other books subsequently and found the same thing: sanitized, euphemistic talk about money that just didn't seem to belong in my world at all. I realized what was missing from all these books: they all seemed to pretend that social class didn't really exist. That in the modern world, we were all starting from the same point, all comfortably middle class and all sharing the same financial problems.

As I grew up I accumulated the knowledge of all the standard budgeting advice. But it never seemed to sink in. Why? Because *my mindset was still poor*. Because I had learnt behaviors and attitudes during my childhood that I hadn't actually shaken yet. The advice books I read conveniently skipped over any of this awkward talk, and so I never got the opportunity to ask myself seriously: how did growing up poor affect my personal finance skills? How was my mindset different from those around me, and those who grew up more comfortably?

Once I asked this question, stuff started to make more sense for me. I soon realized that what was keeping me from making sound financial choices wasn't that I didn't know all the tricks and tips on saving, or how to do my tax or invest wisely. What was keeping me from living the lifestyle I wanted was my *thoughts*. I realized that I differed in the way I thought about things when compared to wealthier people.

I needed to change my habits, and to do that, I needed to change the mindset I held when it came to money. That is what this book is all about. Most budgeting advice is junk because it doesn't take into account that we *aren't* all starting from the same point. In fact, many of us enter into our adult lives with mindsets that almost guarantee we'll stay where we are, making the same mistakes over and over again. The same mistakes our parents made.

In the chapters that follow, I'd like to suggest a way to get to the root of the mindset that may be holding you back, no matter how much well-intentioned advice you follow.

Chapter 2: The Cycle You Never Knew You Were Trapped in

Growing up poor can change the way you think about life. Your parents teach you many things, but you were too young at the time to actively notice it. So, you adopted their version of reality as reality itself and even if you did start to question it, it was well after these associations and beliefs were cemented in your mind.

You may have the belief that you need to lie and be greedy and unethical to succeed in life (did you see your parents denigrate and mock people wealthier than them?). You may believe that people "like you" simply don't ever succeed – or that you do but within very defined limits. You learnt from those around you what to expect from the world, how to behave, what to do in the face of failure, how large your dreams were allowed to be and what it meant to be "rich" or "poor".

The thing is, everything that you learnt is *not* reality – just one version of it.

You know who didn't receive that same version? People who don't share your socioeconomic bracket. People think that the only difference between rich and poor is that wealthier people can afford more things, but this isn't all they can afford. They can afford different *ideas*. They teach their children to expect a lot, to work hard, to automatically assume that something can be done rather than the opposite. We'll get into this idea a little later in the book.

"Poor": An Expanded Definition

But what does it actually mean to be poor, anyway?

I've just been throwing the word around and assuming you know exactly what I'm talking about. But what makes someone "poor" and someone else "rich"?

Every once in a while a politician or public finger finds themselves in the media when people discover just how much their house is worth, how much money they take home every year, or what disgusting amount their wives have spent on designer handbags. The politician jumps in and defends himself: he's *middle class*, you guys. He might even say he grew up poor. He's not rich at all, in fact, after he pays all his staff and employees, he actually has very little left over…

Every once in a while you also read about lifestyles or quality of life in other countries, and are shocked to find out just how little others have, even though they might protest and explain that they are, in fact, quite wealthy. They're *middles class*, they tell you, they have everything they need…

Looking at all of this it's easy to conclude two things: first, that "middle class" is a limbo land and can mean whatever you want it to mean, and second, that poverty is more of a *mindset* than an objective fact.

Poverty is, in fact, a feeling.

Cold hard cash and how much you have of it – this is an objective fact. Whether you have food to put in your mouth and a way to protect yourself from the elements – also an objective fact.

But deciding how successful you are, deciding whether you have "enough" and what that even means, comparing yourself to your peers and your own internal standards, feeling how well your lifestyle supports all your dreams and desires... these things couldn't be any further from objective fact.

The definition of poverty I'm going to be using in this book is the same one *you're* using. Whatever that is.

What "counts" as poor depends on where you live, how you were raised and your own principles. How you define yourself is entirely up to you. My hope is that by the end of this book, you'll be thinking of yourself a little differently. But for now, I want to point out that there's a reason so many people disagree on the definitions of "rich" and "poor": the reason is because there *aren't* any definitions!

One more thing: I'll talk about poverty here in a very broad way. I want to convince you that being "impoverished" is something that extends far, far beyond how much you have in your bank account. Lack of money can be just that, a lack of money. But in the real world, consistently being deprived of the things you need to live your best life can have far-reaching consequences.

You can be impoverished in thought. In the same way that lacking money limits your options for the food or clothing you can buy or the places you can live, it also limits the kind of thoughts you can have. It clips your dreams and your self identity into smaller shapes. In the same way that you might buy lower quality clothes or settle for no-name groceries, you might only be able to "afford" a certain attitude, a certain life philosophy and worldview.

This is what this book is about: being impoverished. Of course, you can add money and hope that everything sorts itself out. But look at "poor" people who win the lottery. They don't suddenly develop a taste for steak and caviar and have the urge to develop their investment portfolio. Their attitude to life remains impoverished.

So, you can be "poor" with a lot of money, or "rich" with much less. Being impoverished, however, goes a little deeper. It's this attitude that's hard to pin down, but once you start looking for it, you'll notice it everywhere. Let me show you what I mean in the next chapter…

Chapter 3: Three Beliefs That Impoverish You

As we've already seen, almost everything we know about money originally came from our parents. They outlined for us all the things that were possible in the world we inhabit. They told us what money was and what it was for, and by watching them, we learnt (or didn't learn!) how to manage it.

If you read the title of this chapter and thought, "nah, I don't have any impoverishing beliefs, after all, I'm just middle class anyway..." then I want to challenge you to keep reading. You might be surprised by what you learn about yourself!

Active or Reactive?

Psychologists call the characteristic that I'm about to talk about "locus of control". Fundamentally, it's all about *where* you see power and control coming from, in your life. It's the way that you answer the question, "who's running the show here?"

So, for example, someone with an internal locus of control might get promoted at work and conclude that *they* are the reason why.

They caused the promotion to happen, they are responsible for it and now they'll take the kudos for it.

A person with an external locus of control, on the other hand, might also get promoted but explain that event in a completely different way. They may believe that they were favored by the higher ups, that they just got lucky this time, or that they've been handed an opportunity by someone other than themselves. It's not their doing, the promotion came from outside somehow.

That seems simple enough, but zoom out a little and think of the biggest possible picture. How does the universe itself work? Where do you fit into it and what causes things to happen to you? In other words, who's running the show?

Even people who are proactive and responsible in their work and life can fall back on worldviews that are very, very different. They may believe that ultimately, they don't really get a say in what happens to them. Whether it's God, or karma, or evil corporations that control the world, the sentiment is the same: their lives are run by things outside of their control.

An impoverished person believes:

- That "old money" dynasties and special secret networks are really controlling all the wealth in the world and you can't do anything about it if you're not a part of that.
- That money has to be *given* to you. That money is a reward you earn from someone who has more than you, in exchange for playing by their rules.
- That there are specific degrees and qualifications that will open doors and whisk you from one income bracket to the next.
- That proper money management is all about passively saving as much money as possible.
- That the way to advance in life is to get more and more prestigious job titles, and own assets and property.

An un-impoverished person thinks:

- That there are rules and hierarchies in the world, but that you don't always have to play by the rules, and if there are any secret inner circles, there's no reason why they can't be part of them.

- That the super wealthy are not some alien species, but just regular people that you could emulate.
- That money has to be *made*. That money is a reward you earn from creating something of value, in exchange for taking risks.
- That education is important, but there are no secret handshakes or degrees that fast track you into success. That learning practical, real-world skills is just as important, and you don't need any institute to validate that learning for you.
- That proper management of money is all about actively enhancing your ability to earn as much as possible. Saving is secondary.
- That the way to advance in life is to gain skills and a mindset that are intrinsically valuable, no matter what.

Ultimately, it's the difference between active and passive. The passive, external locus of control asks, "what are all my limitations here? What rules do I have to follow? What is expected of me and how I can win at the game that others have set up for me?"

The active, internal locus of control asks, "what do I want and how can I get it?"

One is focused on the outside, with all its constraints, and the other on the inside, and everything that you have under your control. One sees wealth as coming from the outside, the other, from the inside. It's the difference between hoping for a good salary and becoming an entrepreneur so you can decide on your income *yourself*.

Logical or Emotional?

As I mentioned before, poverty is a feeling. Wealth, abundance and security are states of mind.

Because of the way less fortunate people are raised (and sadly, this is the case for *most* people!), money becomes a symbol for a whole host of tangled emotions, thoughts, beliefs, expectations and automatic habits. Money becomes a stand in for lots of complicated states of mind: success in life, how you measure up to your peers, your feeling of safety and wellness in the world – it all comes together in this hot button called "money".

Money can be shameful, a source of deep unhappiness and stress, something embarrassing and hard to figure out, something you always want to avoid even thinking about, something that wears you out and saps your joy in life. "Money is the root of all evil".

Because of this, many people have attitudes towards money and those who have it that don't make a lot of sense. Disdain for "snobs" can hide deep insecurity and jealousy. Some people convince themselves that those better off are actually faulty somehow, that they must have gotten their wealth illegitimately or they must lack something special in life, like faith or a happy family. But all these stories and feelings and thoughts are just that: stories.

Having an overly emotional attachment to money makes you all the worse at managing it!

How do wealthier people think about money? Well, they think of it as what it actually is: a tool. A resource. Something to use to allow them to manage the rest of their lives. A thing to manage and moderate, to build, to develop.

It may be unfair, but such people, for whatever reason, lack the strong emotional attachment to money that poorer people have.

They may enjoy their wealth or stress about it occasionally, but nowhere near on the same scale.

Let me make an analogy. A person who has terrible hang ups about their teeth, a fear of needles and no understanding of how the body works will find going to the dentist a really horrific experience. You could probably guess that such a person won't make the best health decisions when it comes to their dental care.

But a person without such hang ups or fears just …goes to the dentist. It's a normal, everyday thing for them. They might not find it totally pleasant, but they just calmly get on with it: what do they need to do? What's the story and how do they fix any problems and move on with the rest of their lives?

This is the way that people without money hang ups behave. Richer people have an ease and familiarity with money that makes them better at managing it. They think about it logically. They don't avoid discussing it, and don't have those burning, unpleasant associations with their self-worth and identity. It's just money. It's a paradox actually: the rich can afford to just chill out and *stop thinking about money* quite as often. It's the poor, paradoxically, that are obsessed with it.

This ties in a little to the previous point – that of control. For wealthier people, money doesn't control them. They control it. For poorer people, money is a big, scary, frightening, exhausting thing that controls them.

Audacious or Doubtful?

I have a friend who is an incredibly talented artist. After much encouragement by others, she decided to try and sell some of her work. But her attitude was always, "nobody likes this kind of thing anyway, nobody will buy it, and I hate the sales and marketing side of things so much that I would probably just mess it all up anyway."

Do you notice the external locus of control? The emotional attitude? My friend also had a third "impoverished belief", namely doubt. What she ended up doing was pricing her work way, way too low. She had internalized the idea that it wasn't worth much, and acted accordingly. She was so doubtful about the possibility of even being a little successful that she acted as though she had already failed. After many people bought her work at the (extremely) low price, it began to make sense to her: why had she settled on this low, arbitrary number for her prices? Why had she immediately put a ceiling on herself?

She thought she'd lose customers if she priced higher. She didn't. So she priced even higher still, always riddled with doubt, as though she couldn't even imagine something other than just getting by or failing outright. But she kept selling. She had an impoverished mindset, and it had been seriously holding her back.

Rich people have a certain audacity about life. They don't even bother with doing what my friend did, they would have dived right in with the *highest* price they could get away with first and watched to see what would happen.

An impoverished person thinks:

- Life is something to survive.
- That the ultimate goal is to be comfortable and not take too many risks.
- That they can only succeed by the kindness of others, by luck,

by being "fortunate" or by convincing others that they're worth it.
- That they need to ask permission, and are just waiting for conditions to improve or for someone else to show them how to succeed.
- That it's arrogant and greedy to always push for more, and you shouldn't go "above your station" and act like someone you're not.

An un-impoverished person thinks:

- That life is something to optimize – and there's always something more to improve on.
- That risk is just part of life!
- That they can succeed if they work at it.
- That they are in charge and don't need anyone's permission to take risks, or make a plan and follow it.
- That if they don't push for more, they won't get it. That they have to be a little uncomfortable and try new things to make money and get what they want.

The "audacity" that wealthier people have is really like an

unshakeable confidence. They believe, more thoroughly than poorer people, that they deserve things and that the only thing standing in their way of getting those things are challenges that are easily surmounted. A rich person doesn't secretly believe that they're unworthy. In fact, it's the opposite; they know that in life they'll get precisely what they fight and work for!

A poor person, on the other hand, is unconfident. They're unsure about life in general, doubtful about their abilities to master it. They assume the world is holding them back and so they behave in ways that *hold themselves back.*

It's a self-fulfilling prophesy that goes like this:

I am not good enough, not like those rich and successful people, so all I can hope for is to survive and make do (and be "middle class"!) as best I can. Life is hard and difficult to figure out, and it's stupid to take risks when just getting by is so difficult already. So I don't take risks and don't step out of line. It's tiring so I'll spend money on entertaining myself and giving myself treats now and then. I'll stay in the hierarchy, take orders and wait for a promotion. Make myself useful to others and the dreams they have for themselves — I can get to your own dream later, when my life doesn't suck as much as it does now...

Such a person makes poor financial decisions, sees the results as proof that their worldview was right all along, and gets themselves stuck in a nice cycle of more and more impoverishment.

A person with less emotional attachment to money, more audacity and an internal locus of control is going to have a totally different thought process going on:

I'd really like to make more money and live a particular kind of lifestyle that I know will support all the dreams and goals I have for myself. That's going to take a lot of work and planning, so I'd better just get used to taking risks and being out of my comfort zone. I'll spend my money on learning as much useful stuff as I can. How can I be better? What needs to be improved on here? I'll keep asking that question and appraise my plan of attack as I go along. My dreams are not going to happen by themselves, and I'll need money to make it all work! I'd better stop wasting time on distractions and focus my energies...

Which person is going to be prepared and ready to strike when opportunity knocks? Which person is going to price their artwork really low and be satisfied with it? Which person will keep on their toes and learn all the skills they need to adapt and thrive and which person is going to believe they deserve a "treat" for surviving a long work day?

"Entertainment" – a trap

Why do people who have less money to spend sometimes buy very expensive sneakers or spend a fortune on things that even wealthier people think is wasteful? If you asked them (or if you do this yourself!) the answer won't be that they're just bad at finances and don't truly understand what they're doing. More likely, the answer will be, "I work so hard all week long. My life is difficult and stressful, just let me have this *one thing…*"

Before we move on to the next chapter, I want to quickly talk about what's so cyclical about the "cycle of poverty" and what exactly you need to be breaking out of. What poorer people "should" spend their money on is understandably a touchy topic. Who are we to tell someone who's scraping by that the few luxuries they have in life are all wrong somehow? If you work a long, hard day and want to come home and veg out with junk food and alcohol, who's to say you don't deserve it?

But this could be the start of a cycle that's difficult to break out of. When life is stressful and uncertain, it's tempting to grab what little scraps of pleasure and relief you can when you can. But these bad habits could eat away at what could otherwise be savings. They could rob you of time you could spend not just recovering from the stress in your life, but actually finding ways to address the root causes of that stress.

Don't be tempted to blow huge amounts of money to soothe yourself from how stressful it was to earn that money! It's like busting your ass at the gym to burn an extra 300 calories, then rewarding yourself later on by scoffing down 600. It's obvious how this can keep you trapped, going round and round and never really getting anywhere. You'll feel like you work yourself to death but never make any progress.

Do you identify with any of this? Perhaps you spend too much money on numbing/distracting yourself from a lifestyle you hate (i.e. "entertainment") instead of stopping, deciding what you actually want and spending your energy and money on making it a reality.

Of course, if you're the kind of person who would be utterly miserable without your little vice (clothes or shoes you can't afford, expensive games or consoles, alcohol, cigarettes or substances, junk food, gambling, beauty treatments and makeup you don't really need…) then you're probably wondering what the hell you're supposed to do without it.

First, divide every task you encounter in life into two categories:

1. maintenance, and
2. growth

Everything you do either keeps things ticking over, just as they are (maintenance) or it actually moves you *forward* somehow, bringing something new and better into your life (growth). When something in your house breaks, and you fix it, it's maintenance. You're just actively working to keep things from getting worse. But if you take an afternoon off and lay in some new tiles on your bathroom floor, that's making a renovation. Things are better now. This is growth.

The reason I make the distinction is because when you're in a cycle of poverty, all your actions are maintenance actions. That's why you get nowhere – there's never any time or money to do growth activities. So you just run and run to stay in the same place. "But I *have to* go to work" you say, and it's true. For most people, sadly, their work is going to be 90 – 100% maintenance, never truly moving them anywhere. And they're so tired after work that they don't have the energy to do any other tasks, like learning something new, bettering themselves, spending time with hobbies or passions or family. A horrible situation to be in!

To break the cycle, make sure you're doing at least one growth activity, every single day. Don't have the time? Have a look at your "entertainment" and you'll find some, I promise. Take the money you spend on junk food, the time you waste in front of the TV, the cash you fritter away on the weekends …all of it adds up and can be put to far better use in a million other ways.

It may be difficult at first because you'll feel like you're losing your "reward", but try to remind yourself that it may take a little effort to break out of the cycle. It's staying in the cycle that's easy!

Trim down your weekend beer habit and spend that money on a weekend programming course instead. Instead of blowing away every windfall you get, put it away in a savings account for something you know will move your life forward – an eventual deposit on a house, education, or tools or equipment that you could start a small business with. Resist the urge to make a mediocre, unfulfilling life more comfortable and instead invest in things you won't get to enjoy for a while, but will pay off eventually.

When you're exhausted after a long day and all you can think about is zoning out in front of TV, eating something nice and falling asleep, try to remember that although it looks like it, this actually *isn't* a reward, or a treat, or a way to spoil yourself. It's just maintenance – and what you are maintaining is a lifestyle that you don't actually enjoy. Spend some time every day on moving things forward.

Though I've mentioned three beliefs here, ultimately, these "impoverished beliefs" come down to one fundamental idea that is much more than just your bank balance. They're the physical manifestation of your worldview, your attitudes made real, out there in the world.

One is rooted in fear and scarcity, the belief that life is just meant to suck a little, and that you can never have it all, never really succeed, never really get what you want. The other is rooted in something far more hopeful: if you are focused, self-aware and work hard, there's no reason why you can't make money work for you, and use it to achieve the things that are important to you.

Chapter 4: What's Your Attitude to Money?

Some of what you've read in the previous chapter may not have seemed relevant …although I'm sure at least some of it hit close to home!

In this chapter, take a good, honest look at where you stand in your attitude towards money right now. From there, you can start to get a clearer idea of the cycles you're trapped in – and how to get out of them!

For this quick quiz, tick all the statements that apply to you. Don't think too hard about it – just answer naturally (and honestly!).

A relationship with money is like any other relationship – 100% unique. So take a few moments to also jot down any thoughts and feelings you have but which aren't listed above. Understanding your strengths and weaknesses when it comes to your finances will make it so much easier to start making changes that count.

Money Personality One: The Dreamer

1. I feel like if I just had $100 000 tomorrow morning, all my life problems would go away
2. My spouse/parents/someone else handles all my financial decisions
3. I often fantasize about a rich lifestyle with all the trimmings, but not so much about the work it would take to make it a reality
4. Deep down, I think that all wealthy and successful people must be awful, although I am very jealous…
5. I'd rather wait for a promotion in my current job than look for a better one
6. Success with money comes down to luck and privilege
7. Marrying well or inheriting a lot of money are core parts of my financial plan for the future
8. I like playing the lottery or gambling
9. I have "expensive tastes" and like the finer things in life
10. If my parents were richer, or if I had been born in a different time or culture, life would have been much, much better than it is now

Can you recognize the external locus of control in The Dreamer's beliefs? For this personality type, money is a wonderful, desirable thing, but it always comes from *outside*. It's always something they have little control over, some magical, faraway thing that they can dream of but can't imagine actually living.

If you've ticked a lot of these beliefs, maybe you flip wistfully through magazines and daydream about all the symbols of a wealthy lifestyle, but never with any firm intention of what it actually means to achieve those dreams. You might shrug and believe that financial security is something for other people, but not you. The Dreamer is walking around with their own internal ceiling: they can visualize all the good things in life they want, but they position themselves well outside of it, looking in, and dreaming. That is, not *doing* anything about it!

Money Personality Two: The Emotional Ostrich

1. I never open my bank statements
2. I'm just not good with money – I've never been good with numbers
3. I pay a lot of money on late fees or overdraft fees…
4. I've always had debt, or I have a lot now
5. I could never be a cut-throat entrepreneur – not in this dog-

eat-dog world!

6. I'd rather live a good life than chase money!
7. I just avoid talking about these kinds of things, to be honest
8. I haven't thought too much about retirement – I can solve that problem when I get there
9. Talking about money is kind of shameful
10. I was never taught anything about money, I've just muddled my way through till now

The Ostrich thinks that money is scary and painful they so if I pretend it doesn't exist, maybe it won't! Behind this personality type's denial is a lot of unbearable emotion – money is somewhere along the line interpreted as threatening, boring, embarrassing or depressing. So they avoid it!

If you've ticked a lot of these, don't worry – I would bet that Ostriches are the most common of these types. Many of us are never taught sound personal finance skills, and had parents and even communities who taught us to fear and avoid taking responsibility for our money. Because the Ostrich avoids engaging with these painful feelings, they also avoid wealthy, successful people, even believing deep down that financial success is bad somehow, and that they never really wanted it anyway…

Money Personality Three: The Big Spender

1. I'd die of embarrassment to let some people know my true spending habits
2. No matter how much money I have, I always seem to run out too soon
3. If I get a windfall, I spend it immediately
4. I love spoiling my friends and family and enjoying the good life
5. It's important for me to be perceived as completely in control financially …even better if people believe I'm quite successful
6. I sometimes try to appear as though I'm wealthier than I actually am
7. I'm an impulse buyer
8. I feel like I'm way, way behind my peers when it comes to finances
9. Fake it till you make it!
10. I have a lush lifestyle and spend heavily, but have few assets and no savings

The Big Spender has a lot in common with the previous types: namely, the external locus of control and the emotional rather than logical attachment to money. But they go a little further, committing only to the *image* of wealth and success, rather than the work and planning that realistically goes into it. The Big Spender values financial success not for its own sake, but because it forms part of their identity. They may "keep up with the Joneses" a lot or live beyond their means.

Money Personality Four: The Money Martyr

1. I often buy something and feel really guilty afterwards
2. My job isn't really going anywhere
3. Even though it makes me feel stingy, I'd do anything to get the best deals or buy the cheapest possible item
4. I often blow a lot of money to de-stress and then regret it later
5. People like me never really get rich, we just get by, and I'm fine with that. After all, what's so special about me that I deserve a fancy life?
6. I find that a lot of my life revolves around stressing about money

7. I never feel secure when it comes to money
8. I don't play the game to win, I play it just to *not* lose!
9. I resent those who seem more successful and happier than I am
10. Life is just one financial obstacle after another, and I almost always lose

Just reading The Money Martyrs list is depressing, don't you think? This personality type sees money as nothing but a massive tormentor. They're slaves in their own lives, hopeless and unable to improve, only ever keeping their heads above water and hating those who seem to find a way out.

This is a pessimistic, limited way of thinking. People with this mindset will never take risks, and will constantly feel like their jobs and finances are something to survive, rather than to thrive within. Money is a source of stress and misery, rather than a practical way to reach your goals. Goals? The martyr doesn't even dare to have goals – they can't afford them!

Money Personality Five: The Confident Realist

1. I have a five-year plan
2. I understand everything that's deducted from my salary and know exactly what I take home each month
3. I can tell you what I spent on entertainment last month
4. I'll be OK financially – I'm not afraid of a few bumps in the road, I always land on my feet, because I'm willing to do what it takes!
5. I think of money as a tool
6. I use the money I earn to pay for a life that makes me happy and fulfilled
7. I always look for opportunities and try to find the bright side in my situation, whatever it is
8. I admire and look up to those who have done better than I have, and I'm really curious about how they did it
9. There are plenty of problems in my life – but I'm bigger than those problems, and I don't let them control me
10. I think of my life in terms of time and value, and not so much in terms of hours worked or what my salary is.

And finally, we get to the *Money Realist*.

These people are quietly optimistic, a little forceful and cocky sometimes, but convinced of their own innate ability to control and determine their own destiny. Such a person doesn't "hope" for anything, take gambles or wish that something would fall in their lap – they simply become curious about opportunities around them and do their damndest to make the best of those, through determined hard work.

This personality may have some emotional associations with money, and they may have hiccups and setbacks like everyone else, but their mindset is fundamentally different. They don't ever question whether they deserve success or security, and they certainly don't ask anyone's permission to do it. They just do it. And they keep on doing it.

How many on this list did you tick?

Chapter 5: Attitudes Lead to Behaviors, which Lead to Attitudes

The point of shining a light on the inner workings of your money-mind is not to feel bad about yourself or shrug and conclude that nothing can be done. Attitudes lead to behavior. And when you behave, you actively change and shape the world around you …which in turn confirms and maintains those same attitudes.

Our attitudes have a way of bringing themselves into being – we can only choose from the options our attitudes have allowed us to notice. When we have a setback, it's our attitude that helps us explain what happened and decide what to do next.

Once you know exactly what thoughts are steering your behavior, you can start getting to the exciting stuff: *changing*. Simply plonking down some new behaviors on top of your old life will never really change much. But if you can dig deep and root out those underlying beliefs that are powering those behaviors, you start making meaningful progress.

Let's say you identified with the Big Spender money personality above. For you, money is like food or love – something you just don't want to put limits on! Your belief may be that we should "eat, drink and be merry, for tomorrow we'll die!" and so whenever you have money, you spend it. All of it. You have the belief that money is for enjoying, but of course, this means that you have no savings, no safety net of any kind, and no strategy for the future.

So when you're faced with that kind of financial insecurity, your belief is confirmed: money can disappear at any time! You had better enjoy it while it lasts! So the next time you get money, you blow it again, celebrating its return into your life. The cycle continues.

Maybe your relationship to money is more like The Emotional Ostrich. Dealing with money is so unpleasant you just ignore it and hope it'll all go away somehow. So, your belief is, "if I close my eyes and shut my ears and don't look at all this scary stuff, it won't exist anymore." Of course, it's a faulty belief. While you're in denial, your finances are doing whatever they're doing, and likely getting worse. Your behavior might lead you to miss important deadlines, fail to notice weird charges or fees that you really should query, file late on your taxes or do it incorrectly, get ripped off when buying things or lose important documents.

The result of this attitude, though, is the opposite of what you hoped: not only do your problems not go away, you're just inviting more and more of them into your life! The cycle continues.

Of course, these are just examples, and your real life will be far more complex, probably with a few elements from more than one type. But that's fine. Though the details may differ here and there, everyone still follows the same principle: your beliefs inform your behavior.

Change the beliefs, and the behaviors will change as well. You can try to force an attitude change by forcing yourself to behave differently (like most personal finance books would suggest) but this is likely to be much less successful!

I'd like to ask you to do an exercise now to try and zoom in on your own beliefs and the behaviors they're keeping in your life. Return to the beliefs you identified for yourself from the last chapter, and choose around three or four of the strongest ones. For example, you could go with:

- I resent those who seem more successful and happier than I am
- I find that a lot of my life revolves around stressing about money
- Even though it makes me feel stingy, I'd do anything to get the best deals or buy the cheapest possible item

Now, you might identify with the The Money Martyr stereotype. Always scrimping and scrooging, letting money (or the lack of it!) completely sap the joy from your life. Now, what are the specific *behaviors* that stem from these attitudes? You could note down:

- Because I resent others who are wealthier and more successful than I am, I avoid them and associate with those like me, or those who are even less successful than I am. I don't seek out those who could teach me something new or offer me new opportunities.
- Because I always stress about money, I try to get relief by not thinking about it, but then problems get out of hand, which cause me more stress anyway, and then I get stuck in a vicious cycle...
- Because I always go for the cheapest option or the best

budget deal, I often drastically reduce my quality of life for very small savings. This depresses me and confirms my belief that I'm not worth nicer things, which makes me less likely to work to bring them into my life.

When you sit down and have a good honest look at your beliefs, you'll probably find that many of them are self-sustaining – in other words, believing them traps you in a vicious cycle that's hard to break free of, so you keep believing them.

In the example above, you can see how stingy, fear-driven beliefs lead to a life that is focused on lack and on reducing. You're always about making things less, about minimizing, about saving and retaining. How could you ever dream big or take risks or be joyfully expressive if all your beliefs are focused on *lack*? When so much doubt controls your life, you don't even entertain the notion that with some effort and risk, things could improve. And so you prove to yourself that the world is harsh and that scarcity and misery are just the norm.

Take some time to really look at the beliefs you hold and how exactly they manifest in your life. If you've held your beliefs for a long time, this may seem difficult. You may be tempted to say, well, this *is* the way things are, this isn't a belief. Fair enough. For now, just become curious about the links between what you believe and what you *do* in the real world because of that belief.

A good way to zoom in on this is to ask, where would you be *without* this belief?

Ask yourself, is your current mindset actually working for you? What would happen if you abandoned it? If you do nothing at all and carry on going as you are, will you be happy with the result a few years down the line?

Chapter 6: This is NOT a Motivational Book

Perhaps you've read this far, and you've identified your blind spots when it comes to thinking about money. Maybe you've been honest and had a good look at the beliefs and feelings that are holding you back from taking financial responsibility in your life. Great. Now what?

There is a dangerous "law of attraction" vibe around personal finance improvement. You're probably already familiar with it: have the right mindset, and the universe will deliver. Just think the right things, truly believe and then wealth and abundance will just rain down onto your lap with no effort.

Do you recognize The Dreamer personality type in this? This is the ultimate in external locus of control. In place of "my boss" or "my father" or "God himself" you have "the universe" and whatever mysterious processes it runs on. You believe that if you just hold thumbs and have the right attitude, you'll be *rewarded* with everything you want and need.

While I want to emphasize just how fundamental mindset truly is,

I also want to emphasize that this attitude is actually quite disempowering. Why? Because attitude alone is not enough. Because nobody gives you the reward but you.

Here are some harsh truths – if you were raised poor, you're starting at a disadvantage. You've been lied to and told that hard work will get you out of the hole, but that might not be true. Or maybe you've been told that you'll never be more than what you are now.

Simply changing your mindset will likely not help. Money and resources are real, and they don't care about your politics, or whatever mystical self-help book you've read, or what you "deserve" or how much you pray.

To be rich, you have to think rich, not because *thinking* means anything, but because it maps onto specific behaviors. In the end, it's all about ACTION.

Money is a deeply emotional topic. It always will be. As you read this book, your head may be swirling with ideas of what you do and don't "deserve" in life, about the morality of greed, of what it really means to add value in life, of give and take, of whether capitalism is evil and whether money corrupts people, of your social status, you gender, your race...

But none of that matters. We could dwell right now on how young women often make poorer financial choices because they unconsciously expect the men in their lives to take care of them. We could consider whether belonging to a disadvantaged class and being poor is really your "fault" and how institutionalized discrimination may have ensured that you were poor before you were even born. We could talk about the death of the middle class or how evil corporations are or how really smart people should unplug form the system and become gypsy entrepreneurs...

But we won't, because none of that matters. None of that is under your control, so while it may be interesting to think about, in the end it doesn't mean much. What matters is the action you take, right now, whatever your circumstances.

And to make sure you're making the best possible choices for yourself and the life you want, you need to look closely and unravel all the beliefs you hold – especially all those that are actively keeping you in a lifestyle you don't want to have.

So, from this point in the book, we'll switch from thinking about thoughts and beliefs, to engaging with the real-life *behaviors* that come with those beliefs. Zoom in and you'll see: being "rich", managing your resources and living a life that fulfils you is nothing more than a habit. People who are financially secure and in control are not any different from you – except in the way they think about things.

Once you've got a thorough understanding of your ideas and beliefs, it's time to dismantle them. In the following chapter, we'll move onto how to start picking out those beliefs and substituting them with ones that will lead to the kind of life you actually want. But a caveat before we start: none of what follows means anything unless you take the time to really ACT.

Even though you might understand an exercise intellectually, or even though it seems simple on the surface, you won't get the true benefit unless you take the leap and bring it to life in the real world. The biggest characteristic missing in the personality types we've discussed, and the biggest antidote to the three beliefs that keep you trapped in unhelpful cycles, is ACTION.

Mindsets are important. But they're important because of what they lead to: beneficial action. If you're committed to making real changes, then let's move on to the next chapter...

Chapter 7: Breaking the Cycle

The way that you tackle your limiting beliefs and behaviors will be specific to you and your unique situation, right now. The advice that follows is general, but try to keep an eye to tailoring everything here to fit your personal situation. Don't get disheartened if something seems not to apply to you, and don't write off advice that seems very obvious or low-level to you.

Each of the following exercises is tailored to fit each of the money personalities, but I suggest looking at all of them anyway, as most people can find something useful from each group.

Breaking the cycle if you're The Dreamer

If you're a dreamer, you may share the very common beliefs that financial success is something lucky that happens to you, or it doesn't, and you don't get much say in the matter. When it comes to explaining financial success, you may point to:

- Genes
- Family wealth

- Luck
- Genius
- Entrepreneurial skills
- Fate
- Something mystical, like God answering your prayers

But the truth is that none of these things has anything to do with how successful you are. How do I know this? In studies and surveys done on the attitudes held by people in different socio-economic brackets, the above beliefs are shared by poorer people …and NOT by wealthier people. Think about it. Holding the above beliefs are strong predictors that you'll stay poor. And of course they are! If you believe that something's out of your control, why bother trying to change it?

The corresponding "rich" beliefs are different. Richer people are more likely to explain financial success by pointing to:

- Hard work
- Creativity
- Being proactive
- Realistic optimism

What's the difference between these two sets of beliefs? One favors ACTION.

If you identified with this personality type and set of beliefs, your challenge will be to find ways to turn your locus of control inward, and remember all the power you have in determining your own fate. There is no master plan, no finance gods or strokes of luck – there is only you and the actions you take for your own life. That's all.

Exercise One: What can I do?

The question "what can I do?" has two parts:

The "I" part and the "do" part. When you ask yourself this question, you're focusing your attention on the only thing you have realistic control over: yourself. You don't waste time dwelling on how your parents screwed you over or whether the government taxes you too much – this is disempowering. Instead, you take control and become curious about *your* scope of influence. No matter how small that may be, *you* own that possibility, and *you* are responsible for taking it – or forfeiting it.

The second part is about doing, about action. To take responsibility for your own role in your future is to become aware of the actions open to you. As we've seen, mindset is nothing without action to bring it to life.

What can you do?

For one day this week, commit to changing your channel from external to internal. Keep asking yourself this question, whenever you're faced with any money decision. Let's say you do some online banking and freak out at some hidden charge you never knew about. You could say, "damn the banks, I hate them, always exploiting the little guys…" and so on. But what good does that do? Nothing. Instead ask, "what can I do?"

This immediately cuts the emotion out, and focuses your attention on what matters: what actions you can take, as the supreme agent of your own life. If there's something you can change to avoid those charges in future, do it. If not, accept it. Keep your mind open for opportunities in the future. Maybe the banks are evil and exploitative. Maybe not. It doesn't matter though ...what can you do?

Try this for a day, and then push it to a week and then longer. See how long you can maintain this frame of mind. And follow through! Once you've identified a course of action, take it and see how different life looks after some proactive choices. When you switch from passive to active, external to internal, suddenly your financial future is completely in your control. Do this with both small and big things and you'll be surprised by how many new ideas and avenues open up to you.

Breaking the cycle if you're an Emotional Ostrich

At the root of the Ostrich's need to live in denial is one very strong emotion: fear.

Many of us are instilled with this fear in childhood. Fear that we'll have to do without. Fear of failure or letting our families down. Fear that money is this big, scary, unmanageable thing that can ruin lives and crush you. If we grew up poor, we may have seen our parents struggle financially. We may have experienced shame in being poor, panic and insecurity over never having enough, neglect or having to watch others experience good fortune while we made do with less.

The irony is that fear keeps the Ostrich in the very cycle they want to escape so badly. By continually engaging with money in fear (and resentment and doubt and all those other nasty emotions) the Ostrich never gets to develop a more neutral, relaxed attitude to money. How do you break out of this cycle?

Exercise Two: Find Your Rock Bottom

Breaking out of this cycle of fear is easy: challenge the underlying fear, and engage with it. For this exercise, you'll need one thing the Ostrich doesn't have: bravery. This exercise will be horrible to do, but that's the point here; you'll dive deep down into the thing you believe is unbearable ...and then bear it!

Wealthier people, especially those who work their way up from poverty, often have a fearlessness to them. They simply *stop caring* about the risks quite as much. They have a "nothing to lose" vibe about them and don't care if they have to suffer a little on the way.

If you read any biographies about supremely successful individuals, they often talk about the early days before they succeeded: bad jobs, scrimping, sacrificing, doing without.

The difference is that they didn't try to *avoid* this state at any cost. Instead of running away from those unpleasant sensations, they dug deep and engaged with them. They didn't enjoy it any more than anyone else, but they looked the hardship square in the face and acknowledged it for what it was. Then they overcame it.

If you identify strongly with the fearful Ostrich, it's time to get over your fear and see that actually, it's not so bad.

In a journal somewhere, take a moment to jot down *the worst thing that could happen*. Enjoy it. Let your imagination run wild. Whatever financial outcome you fear, put it down: bankruptcy, a life of mediocrity, disappointing your family, having no retirement... Dwell on whatever it is that freaks you out and makes you turn your head away whenever you look at it.

Now, ask yourself, is it really so bad?

Is the situation you're imagining really unfixable? Even if the literal worst thing happened, would it be so bad that you couldn't improve on it some way? Often, when you look at your fears up close, you see that they're not really the end of the world. Bad, sure, but nothing you can't survive and deal with. Have you ever heard the saying, "the thing you fear the most has already happened to you"? What's more, your avoidance of that fear could actually have more consequence on your life than that fear ever will.

For this exercise, try to engage instead of avoid. Let's say you receive your bank statement in the mail. You get a sinking feeling and put it aside – you don't want to open it. You don't want to know how bad your debt is getting, how much your overdraft fees are or how much you've overspent this month. Instead of putting your head in the sand, though, deliberately *enjoy* the fear. Go deeper into it. Open your bank statement and revel in whatever is in front of you. Let's say it's bad. Really bad. Let's say your financial life is a total wreck. But again, if even *the worst thing that could happen* is manageable, isn't your current problem even more bearable? Stand there and really feel it: you're still alive, present, aware. You still can make decisions. At any point, you can choose and act. However bad things are, they will end eventually.

Look at the things that scare you. Look at how much you actually earn; look at the exact figure of the debt you owe. Look at how much you're putting away for retirement and how it won't be enough. Take it all in. It's bad? Ok. Fine. It's not the worst thing that could happen, and even if it was, you know that even the worst thing that could happen is manageable. Find that bottom. Be comfortable with it. Know that you can fail even more and you'll still be OK. Fearlessness is not about having no fear – it's more about learning to tolerate that fear, and even thrive with it.

Take a little grit and fearlessness from your wealthier peers: say, to hell with it. When you understand a problem and look at it honestly, you start to dissolve the fear, and dissolve the hold it has on you. And then you can start taking meaningful action. So, do the opposite of what you want to. Go into the fear. See how bad it gets. See that …it's not so bad!

- Print out all your bank statements and take a good look at where your money goes each month, even the embarrassing details you'd rather not admit
- Look at your credit card statements and see how much you

owe and how much you're paying on your debt. Don't try to hide it or minimize it

- Look at your salary and what proportion of it goes to different areas of your life
- When you get that panicky feeling that tells you to turn away, *that's* the place you need to look even closer. Let your avoidance be a signpost for the things you most need to focus on

Breaking the cycle if you're a Big Spender

Big Spenders are somewhere in the middle – they *know* how important it is to take charge of their financial situations and desperately want to. The trouble is the way they approach it. Many cultures emphasize the outward symbols of financial success: expensive assets, a particular lifestyle. It's tempting to imagine that you could access wealth if you could just access the symbols that are *associated* with it. You may be heavily pressured by others and what you "should" be doing in all spheres of life, but perhaps you haven't spent as much time thinking about what money actually means to *you*.

Exercise Three: Find Real Value

A nasty surprise waits in store for the Big Spender: even if they reach a measure of success and financial stability, they realize too late that it all feels kind of empty. Their achievements and possessions might have a sort of "so what?" feel about them. This is because the main driver of the Big Spender's behavior is, you guessed it, *external*.

Instead of deciding on *why* he wants money in his life and *for what* exactly, he's momentarily focused on just getting it. Money is viewed as an end in itself. But then even if you get money, then what? Then you're faced with the question you might have asked yourself in the first place: what is money's true role in your life? What do you VALUE?

For this exercise, you'll take money out of the equation completely. You'll focus instead on a more concrete, more personal question: what actually matters to you? You'll never be wealthy if you can't figure out how to spend your money in ways that benefit your life. What's the point of wealth and security if it never translates into fulfilment and happiness?

You need to stop thinking of money as a goal in itself and start thinking of the overarching goals in your life – those that may or may not need money to be realized.

In a journal somewhere, try to answer the following questions as honestly as possible.

Step one: Identify your values

- What do you care about more than anything else in the world? Family? Behaving ethically? Finding and giving love? Creating? Having fun? Building useful things?
- Think about the times in life you felt happiest, most content and most fulfilled with yourself. What were you doing? Where and with whom? This gives you an idea of what will ultimately satisfy you in life.
- When you're old and on your death bed, and remembering your life, what actions and achievements will allow you to say, "I'm at peace, I did a good job"? Are you doing those things now?

Step two: Are you investing in those values?

Sure, you might spend reasonable amounts during the month and have an exemplary budget. But you're failing hard if there's nothing in your spending habits that supports those things you care most about.

If you value building a loving family and home life, and you spend almost no money on that, your budget and financial habits are not serving you. If you value creativity and expression the most, then why spend most of your resources on things that don't feed that value in any way?

Look closely and you'll realize that nobody has the ultimate value of "I want to appear wealthy to my peers" or "I want to make sure I live in the way that everyone else is living".

- Look at a typical month and what you spend. Visualize the information in many different ways to get a sense of where most of your money (i.e. energy!) is really going. Much of it will be towards keeping you housed and fed, but after that? You may find that mindless entertainment and distraction are not your truest, deepest values, and yet your budget says otherwise! Does your budget support what you ultimately value? If not, it's probably working *against* it.

- How much of what you spend each month is because you should, and how much is because you want to? We all need to pay tax and rent/mortgage. But are you spending money on a big, beautiful home when deep down, you couldn't care less about that kind of thing?
- What percentage of your income is going to actually improving your life? Not just maintaining it, but improving it. Is your lifestyle working to maintain you or are you working to maintain your lifestyle?

Step three: Re-allocate

The best budgeting doesn't require you to cut your spending at all. You only need to *re-allocate* resources you already have. Imagine a person who hates coming home each evening and blowing hours watching Netflix, feeling guilty they do nothing with their lives. They look at their budget, and add up everything they spend on binge eating in front of the couch, watching TV series.

They take that money and pay instead for sewing classes in the evenings. Their net expenditure is the same, but they've added value to their lives: they've put their money where their passion is and made a step towards a lifestyle that fulfils them rather than just keeps them ticking over.

- Take the low hanging fruit first: find those places in your budget that actively undermine your quality of life. Now's the time to quit a wasteful habit, stop smoking or cut down on low-return behaviors like gambling or drinking too much.
- Find places in your budget where you spend money on things you don't actually care about and won't miss if they're gone, or will miss very little.
- Ask yourself, can this money be put to better use somewhere else? What dreams and goals and ideas have gone neglected because you didn't have the time or money? Can you find a way to pout those resources there, instead of into wasting time or buying things you don't want?

If you're a Big Spender, be thankful: you're guided by a real sense that life should be enjoyable, and that you want to enjoy it. Your only challenge is to identify more efficient ways of using the resources you have.

Better yet, find ways to add value to your life that don't include money at all! Big Spenders often build their identities around generosity, but can you show love and celebrate and enjoy life without spending money? Think of places to volunteer, or choose memorable activities to do with loved ones rather than lavishing them with gifts.

The deeper question for someone with this money personality is: *what is truly valuable*? Not what culture tells you to want or what your family and friends pressure you into wanting. But what do *you* want, deep down? And how can you arrange your life in a way that gets you closer to that?

Breaking the cycle if you're a Money Martyr

We've seen that Money Martyrs are all about focusing on *scarcity*. If you grew up poor and watched those around you be tormented by the "root of all evil", you may have developed some pretty dire attitudes towards finances in general. You may have internalized the fact that life is just crappy and you don't dare hope for otherwise. You want to keep your head down, make rent and not get an ulcer from all the stress.

If you try following traditional money advice, you may be tempted to go for the kind that really just tells you how to live on even less. Clip coupons, make extra cheap meals and scrape by with even less money than you do right now. This kind of advice will just bum you out even more, and keep your cycle going.

Exercise Four: Think Big

Martyrs think small. Very small. They ask others what the rules are and then try to do the bare minimum to satisfy those rules so they can carry on with their lives and not think about it again. They don't ever think they can win at life, so they don't try. The world looks like a series of hoops to jump through, bosses to satisfy and bills to pay. What's missing from the Martyrs life? Their *own* dreams.

You may feel browbeaten and exhausted for very good reasons. But at the end of the day, thinking small will never help you. People don't make money or enhance their lifestyles without taking risks, or without having the audacity to ask for more. And really, there's no "asking" at all – rather, there's just taking!

For this exercise, try to invert your natural scarcity mindset. Try to open your mind to another idea: that the world can actually be a wonderfully abundant place, filled with possibility and all the resources you need to build a life you don't just tolerate, but *love*. But nobody will hand it to you. If you decide that you're not worthy of making the effort, then nobody will come along and convince you otherwise.

Go back to the list of beliefs you jotted down for yourself earlier in the book. You can expand on those now or just choose two or three that speak most closely to your experience. Now, have some fun: turn that idea completely on its head.

Let's say you wrote, "People like me never really get rich, we just get by, and I'm fine with that. After all, what's so special about me that I deserve a fancy life?"

Now, invert that belief. Write instead: "People like me can and do get rich, and I'm not happy settling when I know I can do better. I don't need to be special – and I don't need to 'deserve' anything!"

Now, how does that feel, just to say it?

Do this for all the beliefs and thoughts you've jotted down. Where there's apathy, switch it out for audacity and confidence. Where there's a hate and suspicion of wealth and all those who have it, replace it with an attitude of appreciation, curiosity or playful competition. Congratulations – you're on your way to thinking like many "rich" people do!

When you catch yourself in negative self-talk of this kind, switch over to your inverted belief. Now, most importantly, what does that belief lead you to *do*? As we've seen, beliefs on their own mean nothing without the behaviors that manifest them in the real world. As with exercise 1, ask yourself, what can I do?

You may be overwhelmed by this, since it may be the first time you've ever even entertained the idea that you could *do* anything about your situation, but keep asking the question anyway.

When you see "evidence" that your old ways of thinking are true, reject them. Invert your natural tendency to be pessimistic and have the audacity to think something else: you deserve it. You can achieve what you want to. You don't need to wait for permission.

Try replacing your thoughts like this for a few days, but keep coming back to concrete actions, too, for example:

- Look at your job and assess it objectively. Can you do better? Is this really the best job for you right now, and will it grow with you and fulfil you in the long term?
- Instead of saving every last scrap, do you need to focus your attention on earning more? Do you need a raise or a promotion?
- It might be time to upskill and make yourself more valuable in the world (i.e. stop trying to take up less space, but take up more!). Can you take the time to enhance your abilities and gain experience?
- Think about where you'll be in one, two and five years' time. Look at your current lifestyle setup and ask whether it scales up and appreciates over time – or whether it plateaus. What steps can you take now to put yourself in a better position this time next year?

- Raise your prices, ask for a salary increase or invest in buying things that are better quality and not the cheapest. This takes a leap of faith
- When you find yourself stressing about money, stop and become aware of your thoughts for a second. Look and see if your inner dialogue is actually helping you in any way. Are you encouraged to take any beneficial actions? If not, drop the worry and move on with life. Stressing helps nobody and is a waste of your time. Stress only if it propels you into useful action – otherwise, you might as well just relax!
- Ask for help. All those people who you quietly resent for being more successful or financially stable than you? Ask their advice. Or just spend time with them and try to learn what they're doing that you aren't. Compliment those who work hard and take risks. Find a mentor and emulate them
- When you encounter an obstacle, rejoice! Look closely and you'll see that it's just an opportunity in disguise. Every moment in time is an opportunity to learn something, to make money, to hone in on your values or to let go of things that just aren't working. Expect and value negative feedback – and commit to putting it to use
- When you're feeling miserly, double check what's really

causing the scarcity. If you're honest, you may discover that it's only YOU who's limiting and constraining yourself

Chapter 8: Budget Like a Rich Person

When you budget like a poor person (and by now I hope you know exactly what I mean when I talk about a "poor person" – not someone who simply doesn't have that much money, but someone who is stuck in an impoverished mindset, whether they have money or not), you start with your income, minus the expenses, and hope the balance is positive.

You might forget that money is a tool, that it's something there for you to use to enhance your life, your dreams and your goals. You might get trapped in the minutiae like how to shave a few dollars here and there by buying cheaper produce or getting things on sale.

You may focus on lack instead of abundance, on retaining rather than expanding and taking risks. You look at the money you have and ask, "how can I make this go as far as possible?" instead of, "what is the ultimate best use of this money, right now?"

Get cheap – REALLY cheap – with the things that don't matter to you

Common sense tells us to trim away the luxuries first. Get rid of unnecessary spending on fancy coffees or junk food, or little trinkets you fritter your money away on. Right? Actually, this is the wrong way to go about things. What counts as a "luxury" is really only up to you, and even then, the things that give you most pleasure in life are the things you should try hard to *keep* in your budget. Think about it: you get more utility and pleasure from every dollar you spend here than on other things you don't care too much about.

When you're trying to shave down expenses – and there's no shame in needing to do that – start with things that lack a real, subjective value to you. If having the quiet time of a daily coffee ritual is the last thing keeping you sane these days, cutting that spending is a bad move. Instead, look at those things that don't speak to your higher values. If you're going to scrimp, do it on things that don't matter at all. This may not match up with everyone else's idea of what counts as a luxury and what doesn't, but whatever, your budget's not for them.

I know of a guy who couldn't care less about fashion, looking good or fancy clothing. He worked like a dog all through his degree and did it on almost no money because more than anything, he wanted that degree and what it meant for his future. And so he wore, throughout the entire 3 years I knew him, the same two pairs of trousers and the same two shirts. They were identical. While one was getting washed, he wore the other. They had tiny holes in the corners and were pretty ugly, but he didn't care. It was a sacrifice to not buy clothing for years – but a sacrifice he could make easily. He blew his money on gadgets and software and evening classes and conferences. And he went to those conferences in shirts with tiny holes in them.

If you're struggling with money, it'll be so much easier to deal with temporary hardship when you remember that you can *choose where to allocate that hardship*. Keep feeding your passions, and the hardship won't sting that much anyway.

Dream first, then think about the money later

Many people only dream as big as they think they're allowed to. They have an inbuilt "I can't" that they don't even realized they're walking around with. Any financial growth is going to start with a dream that's slightly (or a lot!) larger than the reality you're living in right now. But have the audacity to have that dream anyway, and be curious about how to bring it to life.

Most budgets follow the Money Martyr style of thinking: trim and cut and reduce, at any cost. Of course, the other end of the equation is to think of bringing more *in*. Wealthier people don't stress too much about what they don't have at the moment. They know that resources come and go. They're more concerned with the next opportunity, with finding out which exact path is going to lead them to what they want. Do the same.

Permanently be on a job hunt, and keep feelers out for opportunities at every moment. Are you being compensated properly for your work? Or, are you really adding value to the lives of others? Are you actually *asking* for what you want? So many people just assume they can never negotiate for more money, but why not?

Start with what you want first, and go from there. Don't look around to see all the ways your current situation is lacking and then assume that's proof that you've dreamt too big. Do you remember when you were a little kid and you had grand plans for how you'd live when your parents weren't the boss of you and you could do whatever you wanted? Well, here you are. Time to dream big!

If your dream is large and far away, that's fine. Just identify one thing you *can* do, right now, and get going. You'd be amazed how much time you have when you cut out junk entertainment from your life. And you'd be amazed at how many opportunities you notice when you give yourself permission to accept that they're there at all.

Go back to university. Start your own business. Retire and go backpacking. Ask for a raise. Buy that little thing you want but think you shouldn't get. Or, make any small step in the right direction.

At the end of your life, there's no prize for how well you followed the rules. Nobody is keeping score. The only thing that will matter is whether you can sit with yourself in your last hours and know deep down that you lived well. It won't matter then whether you played it safe. Even reaching for your dreams and failing will seem more valuable to you than never having tried at all.

Stay focused

Think of a budget as a lens that focuses your energy and effort in just the right place. When a laser can concentrate diffuse beams of light into just one point, it becomes really powerful. Do the same. Decide on the goals you value and then tune out everything that distracts you from that. You can waste your whole life "getting ready" or "taking a break" or pputting off things till tomorrow.

Your time, your energy and your money are finite resources. So use them wisely. When you budget, keep other things in mind, not just money. Are you using your time carefully? Are you spending your energy in the right place? Are your actions and movements geared towards what really counts?

If so, it doesn't much matter how much money you have. Money becomes a tool. The question is not, "do I have enough money?" but "do I have enough money to live my values?" When you expand your budget to include your own personal, deeper sense of value, you change on a cognitive and emotional level. You give yourself the chance to step out of self-limiting vicious cycles, and to create a lifestyle that fulfills you. You stop thinking poor.

Conclusion

"We cannot solve our problems with the same thinking we used when we created them."

~ Albert Einstein

I want to end this short book with the same quote I began it with.

Einstein was a brilliant man in part because he was able to think the unthinkable, to push his imagination to places where nobody else's had gone before. He could have been an exemplary scientist by working within the same realm that physicists of his day occupied, and he would have done very well for himself. But he was interested in going a little deeper.

When you become curious about why and how you are all the things you are, you give yourself a great opportunity to truly change. Not just on the surface, but in a more profound way.

Those who grow up impoverished are taught certain attitudes and beliefs that keep them trapped in cycles of behavior that are largely their own doing. If you've always struggled with money, you may have seen something of yourself in the personalities described here. And my hope is that at the very least, I've convinced you that thinking this way is completely, 100% optional.

There are forces that are beyond our control, and political and economic factors that no one person can ever claim to have overcome. We are all part of bigger systems that we don't have perfect knowledge or control over. With money, this is just a fact.

Nevertheless, we always have the power to stop, turn inwards, and become aware of the thoughts and behaviors that we choose to have and which maintain our lives in ways we don't actually want. No matter how much hardship you go through, no matter whether you become very successful or just putter along for the rest of your life, taking responsibility for your mindset will automatically make you "richer" than you were before.

With a clear understanding of what you value, your dreams and your own blind spots, you are prepared, empowered and able to improve your personal finances, no matter what they are. My hope is that this book has encouraged you to think of yourself, and the money you have, a little differently.

Be proactive, be a little audacious, and remember that your dreams are just as valuable as anyone else's.

Take care!

- Simeon

www.ingramcontent.com/pod-product-compliance
Lightning Source LLC
Chambersburg PA
CBHW060406190526
45169CB00002B/782